# COPYRIGHT

# NOTICE OF LIABILITY

# Dedicated to Soapy Friends.

This book is dedicated to my dear "OG" soapy friends who have helped me in my soapmaking journey. All the knowledge I have obtained in this journey is a result of talking with soapmakers, becoming friends with them, and many (many) failed batches of soap. Christina, Kate, Jo, Chass, Ellowyn (and more than I have room to list) ... I never knew being addicted to soap would bring such amazing friends into my life.

To all of those who purchase my soaps, this is for you as well. I feel truly blessed to be a small part of your life with every bar of soap that ships out. I cherish packing gift boxes filled with small delights to brighten the day for your friends and family. And I am excited for those of you who have been inspired to make soap!

Thank you all for becoming a part of my little soapy family.

Now, let's get on with the soapmaking!
Kandra

## *A blossoming friendship with soapers around the world.*

Just a few short weeks after publication, I received multiple requests to create a Facebook group, which then prompted requests for tutorials and other learning opportunities. With encouragement from my sister, and all of the new soapy friends I found as a result of this book, Soapy Friends was born.

Through the website, SoapyFriends.com, the Facebook group, and YouTube channel, I am continually building out new resources for you, my dear soapy friend.

So, what do you say? Want to join me and other soapy friends waiting to meet you and your lovely soaps?

**Visit SoapyFriends.com, or @mysoapyfriends on YouTube, Instagram, and Facebook to join us:**

- Free resources such as updated color charts, and infusion labels
- Live master classes
- Recipes and tutorials
- Weekly live streams on Facebook
- and more!

# CONTENTS

# AN INTRODUCTION
## *(What this Book is Actually About)*

Making soap is a craft, an art, and it's a science. When you add in natural colorants, you expand the possibilities of chemical reactions and become amazed at how low opacity oils can create vibrant pinks, deep and rich mauves turn blue then purple, assumptions are proven wrong, and sometimes even browns become glorious.

For the hobbyist and young soapmaker, a common dilemma is how to re-create something they discovered. As they dive into the art with the craft in mind, and not as a scientist or researcher, they often neglect to record how a particular batch was created. This includes how long infusions were left for, herb to oil ratios, and how much colorant was added (in terms more reproducible than "a bit" or "a good amount"). And yes, I know this because I did the same things!

What this book is really about is sharing my process for experimenting with colorants, how I've created new colors by blending existing ones, and (although not as sexy as the colors) how I take notes and keep records. Luckily, that part is short and sweet. You'll find those details sprinkled throughout the book amongst information about making soap, infusions, soapmaking methods, and a few other tidbits of knowledge that I've gained over my years of soapmaking and conversing with other soapmakers.

Am I a scientist? No, not by formal education. I don't have a degree in sciences (I hold a B.A. in graphic design and communications). But I am a strong believer in self-education. I homeschooled 3 amazing kids with my husband, and I have a deep love and understanding of color through research that stemmed from my grandmother's art studio when I was a child.

This book is also not a one stop resource for making a full rainbow of soap colors. It's intended to give you the tools you need to conduct your own experiments, learn how your infusions react, and how you prefer to do things. There's no one way to make a soap pink, and your technique is what makes your soap unique.

This book is comprised of two main sections: **The Wondrous World of Soap Colors** and **Blending Natural Colors.** I know you'll want to jump right into the 2nd section where the colors appear, but don't be tempted! That would have the same results of cutting your soap too early, you're not going to get what you wanted. In the Wondrous World Of Soap Colors I'll share my methods for infusing colors, when to use water vs. teas or slurries, explain the formula we'll be using (which gives you everything you need to understand how much of each infused oil to use), provide a color chart, and much much more. All of this information is critical to understanding how the color blends are created, and more importantly, how you can create them.

I've also include room in the book for you to add notes about your processes, ratios, and other information you might want to make note of as you complete your experiments. I hope you fill those pages with joy and knowledge and that the process of discovery is as exciting for you as it is for me.

# THE WONDROUS WORLD OF SOAP COLORS

Most commercially available, as well as many handmade soaps are colored with lab-made oxides, micas, and other synthetic colorants. At the beginning of my soapmaking journey, I chose to color soaps with nature. As an artist and painter, I always wanted to explore making my own paints, and as a home school mother had explored natural dyes and inks for science lessons. Most importantly, I wanted to keep this cherished process of making soap as natural as possible. The rainbow hippie in me wouldn't have it any other way.

In order to color soap with botanicals there are a few key points you need to be aware of, and some things that you need to realize you will (mostly) never obtain:

- Nothing is instant.
- There's no glitter in nature, and natural soap will not achieve "neon" colors.
- Colors will change and morph.
- There can be more than one "right way".
- Breath and enjoy what you made.

# Getting Color Out of Nature and Into Your Soap

There are two basic methods to extract color from nature to incorporate it into your soap: using oil or using water. When using oil, we call it creating an oil infusion. When using water, we call it brewing tea, decoctions, or slurry.

An infusion, or maceration, is the process of using a solvent (typically oil or water) to extract molecules (in our case color) from the botanicals. This works because the components of the plant that make the color are "like" your solvent. We know that oil and water don't mix, but if you look at the other side of the equation, oil and oil DO mix. When you infuse herbs in oil, their oil "like" (nonpolar) molecules attract and you end up with an oil infused with the color molecules from the plant. The same goes for water. If the color molecules are "like" water (polar), you will need a polar solvent (i.e. water) to extract the color.

## Oil Infusions (Hot & Cold)

When using an oil as your solvent, you have two basic methods at your disposal: hot or cold infusion. Just as you guessed by their names, a hot infusion uses heat, and cold doesn't.

Hot infusions will give you more immediate results. Cold infusions take time (vs. heat) to extract the molecules from the plant and into the oil. Typically, I find that a long cold infusion is the best choice, while many soapmakers swear by and only use hot infusions.

**Items you need to create a (hot or cold) oil infusion:**

- Clean hands, clean and sterile containers and lids (mason jars are a popular choice)
- A scale
- Plant material and oil at a minimum ratio of 1:15 (that means 1 part plant material for every 15 part oil. For example: 10gr herbs and 150gr oil)

## How to Create a Cold Infusion:

1. Place plant material and oil in a clean and sterile container. Close with a lid.
2. Let the container sit for 4-6 weeks (or longer).
3. Shake the container just enough to agitate for a moment or two, once a week or so.
4. Strain into a new, clean and sterile container.

Note: I have sped up a cold infusion by starting with a hot infusion, then letting the jar sit for 2-3 additional weeks before straining.

## How to Create a Hot Infusion:

1. Place plant material and oil in a clean and sterile container. Close with a lid.
2. To heat your container:

   » Place it in a warm water bath in a crock-pot. The "low" setting is more than adequate.

   » Or, place the container in a warm oven.

3. Keep the container warm until you see your color develop in the oil. This usually takes 4 hours, but I have also let my infusions warm for a full day or overnight.
4. Strain into a new clean and sterile container.

# GOOD NOTE TAKING IS THE KEY TO AN EFFECTIVE SOAPMAKER'S COLOR PALLET.

When you create your infusions, weigh all of your herbs and oils, and record it. I label my infusions with the with the following:

- Tare weight of jar and lid
- Weight of herbs used for the infusion
- Weight of oils
- The Date

I also keep a notebook of how I create my infusions. It's a simple log of how much herb to oil I use, type of infusion (oil, water, slurry, etc), and sorted by color.

You should also note that when creating a hot infusion, it's important to keep the condensation from the water bath out of the oils. This is easily avoided with a well-fitted lid. Speaking of lids, I avoid using the tin lids that come with mason jars and replace them with stainless steel rings and silicon lids. The tin rings and lids can rust and corrode over time.

## Which method is best? That's up to you!

I recommend the following experiment to determine which method you prefer:

Create two infusions with the same dried botanical.

- Process one as a hot infusion.
- Process the other as a cold infusion.

For the hot infusion:

- Pour off enough oil to use in a test batch of soap.
- Leave the plant material in the jar with the remaining oil.
- Let it sit for 3 weeks. Pour off enough oil to make a test batch of soap.
- Do the same thing every week until you are out of oil.

For the cold infusion:

- Let the infusion sit for 4 weeks.
- Pour off enough oil to make a test batch of soap.
- Do the same thing every week until you are out of oil.

# HOW MUCH OIL IS REALLY LEFT IN THAT JAR?

Wonder why I keep the tare weight of the jar and lid on my labels? It's so I know how much oil I have left! To calculate how much oil you have to work with in any jar:

- Weigh your full jar
- Subtract the tare weight of the jar and lid, and herbs if you haven't strained them out yet.

You can either save all of your pour-offs and have a day filled with making test batches (recipe below) or you can make them when you pour off the oil. Either way, take detailed notes and label everything. As the soaps cure, note how the color changes over time, as well as the colors and shades you obtained from each infusion method.

The remaining weight is oil weight. Some of that oil will remain "attached" to the herbs, and while some can be squeezed out, you won't be able to get all of it. Just be aware that you will have a slightly smaller portion of oil available than the actual weight.

## Water Infusions (Teas and Decoctions) and Slurries

Water infusions (teas and decoctions) and slurries, are easily created and are the perfect solution for "I NEED to make soap NOW" moments.

Water infusions (also known as teas) work by extracting water soluble molecules from the plant matter with water. Slurries, on the other hand, work by re-hydrating botanicals (such as spirulina) with water. With a tea, you strain off the botanicals, but with the slurry, you don't.

Many (but not all) water soluble botanicals will eventually result in a brown soap. This is simply due

*Make a tea with delicate herbs like petals and leaves, decoctions with woody herbs like roots and seeds, and slurries to rehydrate botanical powders and clays.*

to the nature of the molecules and their reaction to (or destruction by) the high PH environment of soapmaking.

Depending on the botanical you use, you will either make a tea, a decoction, or a slurry.

**For these methods you need:**

- Clean hands, clean and sterile containers (mason jars are a popular choice)
- A scale
- A pot or pan for heating water.
- Plant material and water.
    - » Teas need about 1-2 tbsp[1] of plant matter per 8 ounces of water.
    - » Decoctions need about 1:16 ratio of plant matter to water.
    - » Slurries take at least equal amounts (by weight) of botanical and water but many botanicals need more (e.g. 10x water for madder root).

**Teas will be used for more delicate herbs like petals and leaves.**

1. Place herbs in your jar.
2. Pour hot (almost boiling) water over the herbs.
3. Let steep until color is released. This will take between 10-30 minutes depending on how strong you would like your brew.
4. Strain your water[2] for use in your soap formula.

---

1  Teas are commonly measured by TBSP (tablespoons) because each herb has a different weight. 10gr of calendula is very different from 10gr of mint. You will want to weigh a tablespoon of your herb and record how many grams were used. Record this data when creating your reference notes for future use. Also note that this amount may vary based on the herb you are using. Some simply require more, while others much less. Remember to take notes as you explore your herbs!

2  Soapmakers often ask if their tap water, or well water, or sea water, etc. is suitable for soapmaking. The answer is always "it depends"... it depends

## A Quick Note on Fresh vs. Dry Botanicals

Most of the botanicals you use will be dried.
However, many soapmakers wonder if they can pick
fresh flowers from their garden and use them in
an infusion. The answer depends on how soon you
will use the infused oil. Fresh plant matter contains
water. Water is a breeding ground for bacteria and
moldy oils. So, if you really want to infuse those fresh
picked dandelions into oil for making soap, process
them with a hot infusion and turn that oil into soap
right away.

**Decoctions will be used for woody herbs like roots and seeds.**

1. Place herbs in in a pot
2. Add your COLD water to the herbs. Let this soak for 2 hours.
3. Turn on the heat and simmer the herbs for 15 minutes.
4. Strain your water for use in your soap formula.

**Slurries are used to rehydrate botanical powders and clays.**

1. Place your powder in a container
2. Slowly add water (hot water works better than cold or room temperature) until you have incorporated the botanicals into the water.
3. Do not strain. This syrupy liquid will be added directly to your soap formula.

## Storing Your Infusions.

**Oil infusions** can be stored on the shelf, preferably in a cool dark and dry location. They will remain viable for the shelf life of the oil used in the fusions.

**Water infusions** on the other hand, should be used immediately or stored in the refrigerator or frozen. This is to prevent bacterial buildup in the high water environment.

- If refrigerating: store in an airtight container (with a label) and use within one week.

---

on what's in your water. For example, hard water contains metals that will promote DOS in soap. I always use distilled water for soap making, and that includes when I make teas destined for soap.

- If freezing: Pour into an ice cube tray (this makes measuring a snap) and use within 6 months. You can store your frozen herbal cubes in any freezer safe container (with a label of course).

## How to incorporate infusions and slurries in your formula.

While infusions and slurries can be added at any time in the soapmaking process, I typically add teas and slurries to the lye solution. Oil infusions are used as all or a portion of the oils required in the formula.

**Teas and Decoctions:** Replace all or a portion of the water required in the recipe with the tea or decoction.

**Slurries:** These are either added to the lye water or to the base oils.

**To add a slurry to your lye solution:** first measure out the water needed for your recipe. Reserve the amount of water you need to dissolve your lye (remember, 1 part water to 1 part lye), then use the remaining water to make the slurry. Add a small amount of water at a time to the botanical powder until you have your desired consistency. Any remaining water can be added to your lye solution. You can then add your slurry to your cooled lye solution, or you might prefer to add it to your batter when:

- you are using the slurry to color only a portion of the batter.

- the botanical in the slurry might accelerate trace. Adding to the batter just before molding could save you from a "soap on a stick blender" moment.

Remember, you need at least an equal amount of water to disolve sodium hydroxide (lye) crystals. If you are using a masterbatched 1:1 lye solution, your slurry will be made with additional water. In order to avoid mushy soap (from too much water) that takes a long time to set up and unmold, keep your TOTAL water (the amount in the lye solution plus any additional liquids) to less than 2:1 water:lye.

**Oil Infusions:** Infused oils can be all, or part of the oils required in your formula. The infused oils are added with your other oils, typically before adding the lye solution. The only exception to this guideline is when making multi-colored soaps. If making a multi-colored soap, infused oils are added to the batter after it is emulsified and portioned out for the colorants. We'll discuss how to do this soon!

## What About Essential Oils?

You will note that the test formula does not use any fragrance or essential oils. This is to avoid discoloration and "misbehaving" soap batter from these additives. Once you understand how your colorants work without additives, you will better understand why they change with additives. It's also best to experiment with as few variables as possible, not to mention that failed batches with expensive essential oils are never any fun.

# Micro Batch Soap Testing

A common question that pops up in soap groups is how small of a batch can you make. My answer is always 100gr! Yup, I often make one bar of soap at a time when experimenting with soap colorants. I'm going to include my recipe for this micro batch, but only if you solemnly swear to only make this itty-bitty batch of soap under the following conditions:

- You have made soap before and are fully aware of how dangerous soapmaking can be.
- You have adequate personal protective gear.
- You have reliable tools, including a thermometer.
- You're aware that this micro batch will give generalization of the color you can achieve in a larger batch of soap.
- You will laugh and giggle if your single bar of soap thickens too quickly (and realize it's because you didn't take accurate readings of either temperature or weight).

Now that we're on the same page, you can also use the same formula to make a 450gr (1 pound) batch for testing. If, like me, you love nicely rounded numbers, let's call it 500gr for 1#, or even better, 1000gr for a 2# batch. These larger batches are much more forgiving than the 100gr micro batch. While they can give more accurate color representations, they are not nearly as cute and you will end up with a lot more soap than you may have a use for.

## First, the Formula:

A formula is a fixed set of ingredients that's scalable. A recipe is a specific amount of ingredients and instructions to make a specific amount of a formula. So, let's understand the formula before we look at the recipes.

The following formula is what I used to create every soap in this book:

- 60% coconut oil
- 10% olive oil
- 10% olive oil
- 10% olive oil
- 10% olive oil
- 1:1 lye to water ratio
- Lye calculated at a 10% super fat.

## The Oils:

I use a high coconut oil amount because it's a white oil which will help me understand how the color works. It is also a low cost and accessible oil. Later on, I can do tests of this color with different oils (that may have their own color tints) to see how they affect the final result.

I use olive oil as it is a readily available and standard soaping oil and it's slower to trace. In the formula, the olive oil is broken out into 4 sets of 10% so I can easily test the amount of infused oil needed to create pastels through more saturated colors (without having to do more math). Examples:

- Make soap with 10% infused olive oil and the remaining 30% non-infused olive oil. Then, make the same soap with 20% infused olive oil, then 30%, then 40%.

- Make soap with 10% EACH of different infused oils to test color blending. Maybe 10% of one, 10% of another, and 20% of un-infused... or 10% of one and 30% of another. This is how we're going to use yellow and blue oils to make green soap!

**The Lye Solution:**

Many soap calculators and soap books provide the amount of water needed to dilute the lye as a percentage of the base oils. This has ALWAYS confused me. And, it really doesn't make sense when you consider that the amount of oil in the recipe has nothing to do with the amount of water needed to dilute the lye.

Other soap calculators and soap books discuss water content based on dilution percentages. I.E. a 40% lye solution, which means your lye water is 40% lye and 60% water. That's better, but percentages sometimes make my brain hurt. (Don't tell my son the math geek!)

My preference is ratios. Why? Because they always make sense and are easy to quickly calculate in your head. And the minimum ratio to fully dissolve lye (sodium hydroxide) in water is 1:1. That's one part water to one part lye.

Water also plays an interesting role in soapmaking. It affects everything from whether the soap will gel (which

# How to Masterbatch Lye (and Why it's Awesome).

Masterbatch simply means pre-mixing so you have something ready to use when you want it. If you masterbatch your lye water, you will always be ready to make soap. And, if you masterbatch at a 1:1 ratio you can account for any additional water (or milks, juices, teas, etc.) by adding it into your recipe. Bonus: if you're aiming to be a full-time mass production soapmaker, your recipes and procedures will be all set for when you can purchase sodium hydroxide in premixed drums.

To masterbatch your lye solution, add equal amounts of sodium hydroxide to distilled water. You will want to add the sodium hydroxide slowly as it will heat up quickly. Also be sure you are using a lye safe container that has a secure lid and can withstand the high heat. Once your lye crystals have dissolved, allow the solution to cool and put the lid on it. Label your container and keep it in a very secure location.

affects the color saturation), to how fast it traces. For this formula, I use 1:1 lye:water for a few reasons:

1. You can masterbatch the lye ahead of time and have a cool room temperature solution ready and waiting.

2. You can always add more water if you would like to slow down trace or explore darkening colors by adding water (thus affecting the gel stage and glycerine).

3. Since we're soaping cool (room temperature to 90 degrees) we won't run into fast trace acceleration from a 1:1 lye:water solution.

**The Super Fat:**

Super fat is the amount of leftover oils that will not saponify (not turn into soap) based on how much lye you formulate with. Example:

- Formulate at 0% superfat and your recipe will have enough lye to saponify all of the oils you use.

- Formulate at 5% superfat and your recipe will have enough lye to saponify all BUT 5% of your oils.

I've formulated this test recipe at 10% superfat for two reasons:

1. With the micro batch recipe, humans will err. With a high 10% superfat, we can err enough to be human and still make usable soap in this super small itty-bitty micro batch.

2. With the high amount of coconut oil in the recipe the soap will be drying. I never like to

# A NOTE ON SUPER FAT

*Super fat is the amount of leftover oils that will not saponify (not turn into soap) based on how much lye you formulate with.*

While a range of 5-8 percent is "normal" for many soapmakers. The exact amount of super fat your formulate for will vary based on personal preference and your oil formulations. For example, soap made with 100% coconut oil is typically supper-fated at 10-20% to account for the drying effect of saponified coconut oil.

waste anything so I do eventually use my test batches! The higher super fat makes these bars suitable for handwashing.

## The Recipes

Now that we understand our formula, let's look at it in a few different recipies (same formula, scaled for different batch sizes).

For each recipe, the instructions are the same:

1. Weigh your oils, lye, and water. You will need a scale capable of measuring in 1-gram increments for the micro batch.

2. In a lye safe container (I use stainless steel or plastic pitchers), add your lye crystals to your water (never add water to lye). Gently stir with a lye safe utensil (I use a silicone spatula) to dissolve. If you're going to make multiple test batches, I recommend masterbatching your lye.

3. Let the lye water cool to room temperature, and no hotter than 90°f and 100°f

4. Warm your oils to between 80°f and 85°f to fully melt the coconut oil. Your container needs to be lye safe, wide enough for your stick blender to fit into, yet narrow enough to fully cover the blades when submerged. For my micro-batch I use a 14oz stainless steel frothing pitcher.

5. Once the lye solution has cooled:

    a. Create your slurries (if using) and add them to the lye solution.

    b. Slowly add the lye solution to your oils.

    c. Hand stir to incorporate.

6. Give the batter a few pulses with your stick blender to ensure that you reach emulsion to light trace.

7. I typically aim for emulsion, then do my dishes while I let the batter thicken up a bit to a thin trace.

8. Pour soap into your molds!

## 100GR MICRO BATCH:

- 60gr Coconut Oil
- 10gr Olive Oil
- 10gr Olive Oil
- 10gr Olive Oil
- 10gr Olive Oil
- 15gr Sodium Hydroxide (lye)
- 15gr Water

# 500gr 1# Batch:

- 300gr Coconut Oil
- 50gr Olive Oil
- 50gr Olive Oil
- 50gr Olive Oil
- 50gr Olive Oil
- 73gr Sodium Hydroxide (lye)
- 73gr Water

# 1000gr 2# Batch:

Each batch of soap made for this book was created with this 1000gr recipie.

- 600gr Coconut Oil
- 100gr Olive Oil
- 100gr Olive Oil
- 100gr Olive Oil
- 100gr Olive Oil
- 146gr Sodium Hydroxide (lye)
- 146gr Water

# A NOT SO SHORT SIDEBAR: HOT PROCESS VS. COLD PROCESS SOAPMAKING (AND THE GEL STAGE)

Cold process (CP) soapmaking is what "most" soapmakers do. The general process consists of measuring your ingredients, blending your oils, adding the lye solution, and bring your soap batter to a trace. You then pour your batter into a mold. Once in the mold, the soap will saponify slowly over 1-2 days.

Hot process (HP) soapmaking is similar to cold process, except you add heat - typically in a crockpot, but you can also use a stove top, an oven, or an industrial hot pot. You measure your ingredients, heat your oils, add your lye to the oils, and mix them together. Heat speeds up the saponification process, and the soap is molded after it's saponified. What's extremely appealing about HP soap is that after the soap is saponified (yet before you mold it) you can add in your "extra goodies" such as a specific super fat, or more volatile essential oils that would not have survived the saponification process.

**With cold process soap**, the temperatures can be cooler or hotter. The soap can gel, or not gel based on how you insulate (or not) your mold and the chemical reactions of your additives.

**With hot process soap,** your recipe will always gel and temperatures used in the recipe may not be as critical.

**The gel stage in soapmaking** is when the soap batter has heated enough to change the crystalline structure of the molecules. This is guaranteed to happen with the added heat in HP soap, and sometimes happens in CP soap. If your soap gels, the colors can be deeper and richer. This includes the "cream" or "neutral" color of the base oils in the recipe.

# Natural Color Chart

The following chart is by no means a complete and comprehensive list of everything soapy-colored, but I hope it provides enough insight to inspire your soaping journey, without becoming overwhelmed. Each colorant is listed by hue and includes notes on how to use it (oil infusion, tea, slurry, etc.)

This chart only lists un-blended colorants (i.e. in the green section, I do list spirulina, but I have not listed the blends that we'll explore next).

I also encourage you to expand the cart with your own custom blends and knowledge:

| | | |
|---|---|---|
| **Yellow Dock** *(Rumex crispus)* | Oil infused | Provides shades of pink. Seems to be temperature sensitive and fades to tans and browns. |
| **Madder** Root *(Rubia Tinctorum)* | Slurry in lye water | Provides shades of pink to deep mauve. Has good staying power. |
| **Himalayan Rhubarb** *(Rheum Emodi) Powder* | Oil infused | Provides shades of pink to rich mauve. Behaves much like Yellow Dock and seems to be very temperature sensitive. |
| **Paprika** | Oil infused. Slurry in lye water | Creates shades of peach to orange. Has good staying power. |
| **Turmeric** *(Curcumin)* | Slurry added to oils | Golden orange. Has a good staying power. |
| **Annatto** *(Bixa Orelana)* | Oil Infused | Provides shades of yellow to orange. It will fade. I've had yellows fade to white within a week and oranges fade to white after 8-12 months. |
| **Nettle, Alfalfa,** *or other green leaves* | Infused in oil, can also work in slurries. | Green herbs will lend a lovely shade of green to your soap. However, they all tend to fade to hues ranging from white to brown to cream or very pale green. |
| **Indigo** *(Indigofera tinctoria)* | Slurry added to oils | The unprocessed plant provides shades of green. This has moderate staying powers, tends to fade to a muted brown-green. |
| **Spirulina** *(Spirulina Platensis) Powder* | Slurry added to oils | Create a wonderful green that unfortunately fades when exposed to light. If you keep your soap tucked away in a cool dark closet though, you'll have green for a year or longer! |
| **Chlorella** *(Chlorella vulgaris)* | Slurry added to oils | Provides a green to blue-green that can fade to gray-blues. |

| | | |
|---|---|---|
| **Indigo**<br>(*Indigofera tinctoria*) | Tea or Oil infusion | The processed plant results in a blue powder that provides shades of blue. I've had wonderful results with both methods, however adding the tea to the lye water always results in accelerated trace. Adding an infused oil seems to behave better for me. |
| **Alkanet**<br>(*Alkanna Tinctoria*)<br>*Root* | Oil Infused | Provides shades of gray to royal purple. A high quality herb and a long cold infusion is required to get accurate and consistent results. |
| **Activated**<br><br>**Charcoal** | Slurry added to oils | Results in pale gray to dark black with the darker blacks tending to create messy bubbles and stained washcloths.<br><br>Also note that there are different types of charcoal: hardwood, bamboo, and coconut. We'll explore hardwood and coconut husk in this book. |
| **Your soap base** | | Soap can have a lovely white, ivory, or cream color depending on the oils you use in your formulation. If your oils are more on the green side (extra virgin olive oil for example) your soap will have a yellow to green hue, which can result in a "purple" turning "brown". On the other hand, light oils (like coconut oil) produce bright whites which will allow your color additives to really shine through. |

# Be a "Good" Soapmaker and Scientist - Record Your Results

As you progress through your soapmaking journey, you will quickly realize that you can't remember everything. Notes, copious and detailed notes, are going to be your best friend. Taking notes doesn't have to be hard or fancy, just accurate and accessible.

When I first started soaping, I had a three-ring binder (which I still have) filled with recipes and notes. Then, I started using spreadsheets, and eventually started using a dedicated software program. Even with the software, I still print out each recipe and record notes by hand while I'm working and after the soap is in the mold. These are later transferred into the software program.

Here are the items that have helped me re-create consistent colors from one year to the next.

- Colorant: source, amount, and method.
- Room temperature: this will have an impact on how your soap sets up in the mold.
- Essential oils and other additives: source, amount, and stage when added.
- Temperatures of both your oils and your lye solution at the time you add the lye solution to the oils.
- Time blending and method (how long you hand stirred, how long you blended with the stick blender).
- Mold type and insulation method. This will help you determine if the soap gelled or not.

# Blending Natural Colors

The challenging colors noted in the previous chart are what inspired me to write this book. Greens fade. Blue is super finicky. Purples are hard to keep consistent. And oranges often fade to yellow. So, what's a soapmaker to do?

One day while making soap, and struggling with obtaining the perfect purple, I thought back to my days in art class studying pigments and primary and secondary colors and I had a thought. Why not blend botanicals in soap the same way I would with paint? Talk about a big light bulb, or rather, soap bubble moment! Here's where this book gets really exciting. Making a green soap that stays green, a black soap that's really black without black suds, an orange that doesn't fade to yellow... all through blending.

*Before we get started, it's important to remember those few points from the beginning of our journey:*

**Nothing is instant.** Many colors require infusions, but we're going to try to "cheat" that a bit by blending and minimizing the number of infusions required to have a full color pallet for soapmaking.

**There's no glitter in nature and natural soap will not achieve "neon" colors.** Some colors will be very vibrant, some will be a bit muted vs. a synthetic alternative, but that's OK! Just be thrilled with what you can achieve.

**Colors will change and morph.** While the intent is to create colors that will "stick" (vs. fade by the time the soap is ready for use), it's important to note that many natural colorants will fade over time, regardless of how you create them. While others will last for years.

**There's no one way to do anything.** The following pages are meant to give you inspiration, skills, and tools you need to, explore natural colors for yourself. The process is long, fun, and extremely rewarding. I'm jealous that you haven't completed it yet!

**Breath and enjoy what you made.** Making soap can be a moment of peace and joy for the soapmaker. Even if things go wrong and you think the "batch is ruined", there's always something to learn from the process. Find that one thing to learn, write it down, and realize you just achieved a very important goal... to continually gain knowledge.

## Here's a quick look at all of the soap colors we're about to explore:

*Ready. Set. Soap!*

# GREEN slurries and blends

One of the "dreams" of many natural soapmakers is a green that lasts. A green that can be kept out in the sunshine for all to see. Ahhhh the dreams. Most natural greens tend to fade. Many soapmakers speculate that it's for the same reason why leaves change color in the fall. As the summer comes to an end, the plant is signaled to stop producing chlorophyll. This allows the yellows, reds, and oranges in the plant to become visible. As to why the chlorophyll tends to fade in soap, my unscientific assumption is that the crystallization process that happens as soap cures breaks up the organic bonds of the chlorophyll. When that happens, the chlorophyll no longer absorbs the red and blue wavelengths that allow humans to see the color green. Whatever the exact reason, we know that "most" natural greens tend to fade.

Remember your first lesson in color science? Yellow and Blue make Green! So, why don't we blend our own green and create a soap that contains components that retain their ability to absorb red and blue wavelengths?

Throughout the book I'll be including pictures of the soaps I made. The mandala mold and the bars are from the same batch. The bars were poured into a loaf which gelled while the mandalas are single cavity molds that did not gel all the way through. It was a hot summer when these soaps were made so the ambient room temperature fluctuated greatly. This made for some rather beautiful and interesting soap tops (the portion exposed to air), and lighter soaps from the single cavity mandala molds.

*Let's dive into our first soapy color experiment and see what happens!*

**First, let's make our base soap with no additives.** This will help us understand what the actual color looks like (plus white soap is so pretty). Reference the recipes provide in previous chapters and make one bar or batch of soap with straight (uncolored/no infusion) olive oil for each of the 10% olive oils in the formula. Here's my base soap, made with the 1000gr recipe, and no additives.

**Next, let's make spirulina and chlorella soap to see how green additives behave.** For both of these additives, we will create a water slurry to incorporate them into our soap.

**Spirulina slurry soap:** Made with the 1000gr recipe, 15gr spirulina slurried with 30gr water, to which I added the 1:1 lye solution.

15 GR.
SPIRULINA

SAMPLES FROM THE BOOK
NATURAL SOAP
COLOR PALETTE
1.2OZ (34GR)

**Chlorella slurry soap:** Made with the 1000gr recipe, 15gr chlorella slurried with 30gr water, to which I added the 1:1 lye solution.

**Now, let's look at a yellow and a blue colorant.** As we'll be using these to blend our greens we'll want to see what we're blending.

**Yellow created with 10% annatto infused olive oil.**

Darker yellow from 20% annatto infused olive oil.

**Blue created with 10% indigo infused olive oil.** Darker blue created with 20% indigo infused olive oil.

Notice the swirls and light "clouds" on top of these bars? That's due to a high-water amount. I added additional water in these batches (and the correlating green blends that we'll see next) to show you how water can affect the final soap. It creates such a lovely cloud effect in blue soaps! These were made with a total water amount of 1.75:1 water:lye.

**Finally, let's blend our staying greens.** You can of course create as many blends as you wish, and I'm only showing you three possibilities. To blend your soaps, simply use an infused oil as any of the four 10% portions of olive oil in the base recipe.

Pictured below are three blends using 10-20% Annatto, 10-20% Indigo, and the remaining olive oil uncolored. Note the "clouds" from glycerin rivers from the high-water content in the center bar.

## Now, let's compare all of our green soaps...

All soaps in this book soaps were made 2 months prior to being photographed. They were all stored in a dark closet to cure. With a zero-light exposure cure the chlorella is holding up well and creates a wonderful dark green. The spirulina is already starting to turn brown. And, our lovely blended greens are holding true to their original color!

# FIND YOUR GREEN

Complete the following experiments:

- ☐ **Create a soap with alfalfa infused oil.** Record your usage rates.

- ☐ **Create a soap with unprocessed indigo powder.** Record your usage rates.

- ☐ **Create a soap with spirulina or chlorella.** Record your usage rates.

- ☐ **Create a green soap with a blended green (yellow and blue).** Record your usage rates.

Once you make your soaps, let them cure for a few weeks in a dark room. Then, take out one bar from each batch and let it sit in all it's green glory exposed to light for a few weeks. Take note of the color change!

After 6 months or so (sooner if your soaps are exposed to bright lights on a daily basis) you'll notice that Annatto at lighter percentages starts to noticeably fade. For this reason, I make green soaps with annatto and carrots (we'll be blending with carrots next!) for the yellow and range from 20-30% indigo for the blue. I encourage you to experiment with different percentages and combinations of various yellow to find your perfect green.

# ORANGE infusions and carrots

I think orange is one of the easiest colors to achieve with natural colorants. Annatto is a tried and true additive; as are turmeric, paprika, and even calendula for lighter yellows. I love annatto for how accessible and affordable it is. And you can top off your jar for multiple infusions with the same seeds, but it has a tendency to fade when exposed to light.

Years ago I gave a bar of soap to another soapy friend (it was a soap swap! I highly recommend that you all find a soapy friend and trade soaps. You learn so much from other soapmakers). About a year later she asked if it was normal for natural colorants to fade. Apparently, she left the soap out on her desk to look at each day (how sweet!) but the design eventually faded after daily exposure to light.

I've found this to be true for lower amounts (anything less than 20%). Your oranges will fade to yellow and then to white. At amounts of 10% or less (a 5% will give you a lovely yellow), your soap will fade to white in 4-6 weeks. Does this mean we shouldn't use annatto? Heck no! It just means we should blend it to maximize staying power.

I've experimented with paprika and turmeric blended with annatto, but my favorite for a true orange is carrots. Carrots also add bubbles, a silky lather, and label appeal if you're selling your soap.

Here are a few soaps with various amounts of annatto, and one boosted with carrots.

From left to right: 10% Annatto infused oils; 10% Annatto infused oils with carrot puree (120gr pureed carrots added to a 1000gr recipe); 20% Annatto infused oils, 40% Annatto infused oils.

Let's look at the carrot and 10% annatto soaps again... after they were left in a windowsill for 2 weeks. This was done to simulate the fading my friend experienced in her soap. I know no one will really leave a bar of soap on a windowsill!

As you can see, the 10% annatto bar has faded quite a bit but the bar with the added carrots is still a sunny orange with overall far less fading.

Here's another set of color experiments from a few years ago with paprika that may be of interest. They involve paprika and madder root at various amounts and show how fading affects the final soap color.

These soaps were made with the 100gr micro batch. The percentages listed are percent of infused oil in each bar. The mandala molds included a 0.5% madder root slurry.

And here they are at 6 weeks old. They were all cured in a closet. The orange from the paprika and annatto is so cheery, and the madder root gives such a lovely coral shade! You notice that the 10% infusion faded to where here as well.

If you're wondering why the moons have damaged areas... This is what happens if your silicone molds are not completely dry when you use them ;)

# FIND YOUR ORANGE

Complete the following experiments:

- ❏ **Create a series of soaps with various amounts of annatto infused oils.** Record your usage rates. Observe the color of the wet soap vs. cut vs. cured for 1, 3, and 6 months.

- ❏ **Create a soap with annatto infused oils, blended with carrots.** Record your usage rates. Observe the color of the wet soap vs. cut vs. cured for 1, 3, and 6 months.

- ❏ **Create an experiment to test turmeric or paprika in your soaps.** Record your usage rates. Observe the color of the wet soap vs. cut vs. cured for 1, 3, and 6 months.

- ❏ **Create an experiment to test blending turmeric or paprika with annatto.** Record your usage rates. Observe the color of the wet soap vs. cut vs. cured for 1, 3, and 6 months.

# PURPLE making the "anti-alkanet"

Ahhh purple. The royal color that represents calm, wisdom, deviation, extravagance… and is the color of lavender. It's one of the most challenging colors to achieve, and it took me over 3 years of trial and errors to be able to achieve a good purple. I was fortunate enough to have a color queen for a friend, Jo Hausler. We spent many evenings chatting and trying to determine what exactly was going on with my alkanet.

Here's a quick recap of the years' worth of attempts:

- Maybe I wasn't infusing enough alkanet
- Maybe my olive oil was too green
- Maybe my infusion wasn't long enough
- Maybe my alkanet was old

I was finally able to get a real purple from alkanet by purchasing quality powdered alkanet root. The big takeaway is your herbs are important! Old herbs can have a negative impact on your infusions.

After successfully making alkanet purple for a few years, I still run into issues with it. Don't get me wrong, it's one of my favorite botanicals. It's so magical how the infusion turns into something that looks like grape juice concentrate, all sticky and lovely. Then turns shades of mauve to blue as you add the lye solution, and finally settles into an amazing purple after the soap cures. But, golly gee willikers, I want a consistent purple!

Before I "mastered" (I use that term very lightly) alkanet, I found a purple that was always purple, didn't require an infusion, and made me consistently happy with each perfectly purple batch. Let's see what this magical purple powder is, and blend up some purple soap!

**First, Alkanet.** If you haven't used it before, you're in for a treat as you watch the colors change before your eyes. Lucky you! (Pictured below: Base formula with 20% alkanet infused oil.)

**Next, we're going to look at Madder Root.** I know, it's not purple, it's pink. That's OK. We're going to blend it, so let's see what it looks like by itself.

Madder root is water soluble, so we're going to create a slurry. I'm going to use the oil weight of the recipe to determine how much of the dry herb to use, allowing us to create a measurement that's easily scalable. The soap pictured below was created with a slurry of madder root using 1% of the oil weight. The slurry was then added to the lye solution. Meaning, for 1000gr of oils, I created a water-based slurry of 10gr (1% of 1000) madder root. If I want to create this exact same color in a 10,000gr batch, I can easily calculate the math to scale the formula to a larger recipe. I recommend that you make a few different batches of madder root so you can see the full range of pinks to mauves you can achieve with this colorant.

**Now, let's talk about the blends.** As I mentioned earlier, this concept started when I was struggling with alkanet. While using madder root for another soap, I contemplated how the lovely maroon slurry looked similar to the alkanet infusions and I flashed back to art school. Surely, I can blend some sort of purple, right? If this madder root was just a bit darker, maybe with a tint of blue, would that make purple? Let's find out!

We're going to use two additional powders in this experiment:

1. Processed indigo (the blue kind)

2. Coconut charcoal (skim ahead to the black pages if you're wondering about the different kinds of charcoal).

I chose to use powders as the alkanet infusion was giving me so many issues. And, as I was determined to figure out alkanet, I didn't see the need for a 2nd purple infusion.

Each of the following soaps were made with the 1000gr recipe.

- 0.3% madder root with 1/8tsp charcoal, slurried with 40gr water, to which I added the lye solution.

- 1% madder root with 1/2tsp powdered blue indigo, slurried with 40gr boiling water and cooled to room temperature, to which I added the lye solution

- 1% madder root with ½ tsp charcoal, slurried with 40gr water, to which I added the lye solution
- 0.5% madder root with ½ tsp charcoal, slurried with 40gr water, to which I added the lye solution

And we have purples! I was so excited when I made my first madder root purple, and I hope you are just as excited. What didn't thrill me was the "tsp" measurements that I was using. How the heck can we scale up tsp accurately? We can't really. But what we can do is make a pre-mixed blend with the same ratios.

**Kandra's top secret purple powder (aka The Anti-Alkanet)**

- 24gr madder root
- 1gr coconut charcoal

It's fascinating that this murky brown powder and slurry makes a purple soap! Use this as a ratio to oil weight for any recipe. The more you use, the deeper and darker your purple will be. I can't wait to see all of your lovely purple soaps!

## *More adventures with alkanet.*

While making this book I had a request for purple soap with alkanet. I was laughing at the entire process as the soaps were obviously going to turn out gray (which happens when either your alkanet is old, or you are not using enough alkanet).

I then make a new infusion, "cheated" it by heating it for a day then letting it sit for 3 weeks. The soap indeed turned purple, but not as intense as I wanted. I was so pleased that I was back to purple alkanet, but wanted more purple (purple addiction maybe?).

I thought that I might try one more batch, but as salt bars for my sister. I was floored at how blue the soaps were! They eventually morphed into blue-purple soaps... now I'll have to embark on another soapy journey with colors and salts!

# FIND YOUR PURPLE

Complete the following experiments:

❑ **Create a series of soaps using varying amounts of madder root and activated charcoal.** Record your usage rates. Observe the color of the wet soap vs. cut vs. cured for 1, 3, and 6 months.

❑ **Create a series of soaps using varying amounts of alkanet infused oil.** Record your usage rates. Observe the color of the wet soap vs. cut vs. cured for 1, 3, and 6 months.

❑ **Try blending alkanet with a small percentage of charcoal to create a deeper purple.** Record your usage rates. Observe the color of the wet soap vs. cut vs. cured for 1, 3, and 6 months.

❑ **Make a salt bar using alkanet infused oil.** Record your usage rates. Observe the color of the wet soap vs. cut vs. cured for 1, 3, and 6 months.

# BLACKS charcoal, more charcoal, and a bit of indigo

In color theory, black is the absence of light. If something is black, it means that it absorbs all the wavelengths of light and prevents it from bouncing into your eye. That's why you can't see in a dark (black) room. To make black soap, the go to, and obvious choice is activated charcoal. The most common struggles soapmakers run into with charcoal are black lather (from adding too much) or gray soap when they were aiming for black (not adding enough, or adding the wrong kind of charcoal).

There are three types of activated charcoal on the market: Hardwood, Bamboo, and Coconut Husk... and they are not all equally black when making soap.

Hardwood charcoal has a larger pore structure than coconut or bamboo charcoal. This makes it great for removing stains, but it's also (in my unscientific assumption) the reason why it makes gray soap.

In soap forums, I've seen pictures of blue(ish) charcoal soaps. I think they are bamboo charcoal, but I have never used it. They could also be hardwood charcoals from different woods.

Let's look at a few examples of charcoal soaps for reference. Both coconut and hardwood, and some with a bit of indigo added to see if we could pull out some blue from either type. I hope they inspire you to explore the various shades from steel gray to midnight blacks you can obtain from charcoal, as well as the range of saturations you can achieve from adding a bit of charcoal to other colors (much like we did with the purple madder root).

These soaps were all made with the 1000gr base recipe. The charcoal was added directly to the base oils and blended in prior to adding the lye solution. The indigo was added as a slurry made with boiling water then allowed to cool, to which I added the masterbatched lye solution.

**Coconut Charcoal Soaps:** ½ tsp Coconut charcoal with ½ tsp indigo; 1tsp Coconut Charcoal; 2 tsp Coconut Charcoal (you can see that it's no blacker than the 1tsp batch but will make a goopy black mess of your washcloth and soap dishes!)

**Hardwood Charcoal Soaps:** 1tsp Hardwood Charcoal;
1tsp Hardwood Charcoal with ½ tsp indigo powder.

Here's a grouping of all of the charcoal sample soaps.

As you can see, the coconut charcoal makes a nice black soap, with minimal charcoal used. The hardwood soaps are grayer, leaning towards a blue-ish hue. The indigo addition didn't do much, but it would be worth exploring more indigo and charcoal blends.

# Find Your Black

Complete the following experiments:

❑ **Create a series of soaps using varying amounts of coconut activated charcoal.** Record your usage rates. Observe the color of the wet soap vs. cut vs. cured for 1, 3, and 6 months.

❑ **Create a series of soaps using varying amounts of hardwood activated charcoal.** Record your usage rates. Observe the color of the wet soap vs. cut vs. cured for 1, 3, and 6 months.

❑ **Create a black blend using activated charcoal and another color (such as blue).** Record your usage rates. Observe the color of the wet soap vs. cut vs. cured for 1, 3, and 6 months. Compare this color to the same usage rate from your original series.

❑ **Create a black blend using activated charcoal and another additive (such as oatmeal).** Record your usage rates. Observe the color of the wet soap vs. cut vs. cured for 1, 3, and 6 months. Compare this color to the same usage rate from your original series.

# WHITE avoiding color and gel

How to get the whitest of white is a question that always seems to pop up in my soapmaking circles. While there is no infusion or tea or slurry, that I'm aware of, to make soap whiter (while avoiding synthetic additives), I did want to spend just a moment talking about white soap.

As mentioned in the color chart, using light oils is key to obtaining a white soap. If you want "heck yes that's white!", make a 100% coconut oil soap. Some skin types will hate this soap, but it will be very white. While I don't soap with animal fats, I've been told that lard makes a lovely white soap as well.

The other option is to prevent the soap from entering a gel stage.

- You will want to keep the soap cool (no higher than 95°F, and 85-90 is even better),
- use as little water as possible (high water soaps always gel, so the more water you add the darker your base will be),
- and put your mold in a cool environment to saponify.

Here's the base uncolored soap from the formula we've been using in this book, compared to my 100% coconut oil utility soap that I use for dishes and general house scrubbing. As you can see, the base formula we've been using has a bit of a yellow tint to it whereas the 100% coconut oil soap is white as white can be. The yellowing in our base formula is from the olive oil. The whiter your oils are, the whiter your soap will be. The lower temperature that you soap at (thus avoiding gel stage) the lighter your soap will be.

**One final note:** The yellow from our base recipe will vary depending on the color of your olive oil. And these soaps will fade to a whiter hue after 3-4 months. A great experiment for every soapmaker to do is make 100% olive oil soap. Make at least a 1000gr batch. If you're up for a more in-depth experiment, make two batches: one with 1:1 water:lye and another with 1.5:1 water to lye. Then, watch as the color changes over the course of a year. You will also notice the lather significantly change as the soap cures over the year.

# Find Your White

Complete the following experiments:

- ❏ **Create a micro batch of soap (one bar) using your standard formula.**

- ❏ **Create a micro batch of soap (one bar) using 100% of a single oil for each oil in your formula.** Example: 1 bar of 100% coconut oil, 1 bar of 100% olive oil.

- ❏ **Create a micro batch of soap (one bar) using your standard formula with a 1:1 water:lye ratio.**

- ❏ **Create a micro batch of soap (one bar) using your standard formula with a 1.5:1 water:lye ratio.**

- ❏ **When creating all of the above, consider making 2 bars and force a one to go through the gel stage with CPOP (cold process oven process) and preventing gel in the other bar.**

- ❏ **Compare your whites.** Once all of the soaps are completed, observe and make notes:

  - Did the increased water change the color of your white?

  - Do you need to alter your recipe for a "better" white? If so, consider reducing the amount of the darker oils in your formula referencing your single oil bars.

  - Did gel vs. non-gel change your white?

# Common Soapmaking Terms

Finally, I would like to leave you with a short list of common terms that are tossed around the soapmaking world. Understanding the "lingo" of any group or community helps others know you're "one of the pack", helps you follow a conversation, and saves you a bit of time when taking notes.

**DOS** - Dreaded Orange Spots. DOS happens (we think) when unsaponified oils in the soap become rancid or oxidize. This results in unsightly orange spots on the bar.

**CO** - Coconut Oil

**CP** - Cold Process

**CPOP** - Cold Process Oven Process. This is making cold process soap, then placing the mold in a warm oven to force a gel. Typically you preheat the oven to its lowest setting while making the soap. Turn the oven off, then place your molded soap in the oven.

**EO** - Essential Oil

**EVOO** - Extra Virgin Olive Oil

**FO** - Fragrance Oil

**HP** - Hot Process

**HTHP** - High Temperature Hot Process. While hot process soap is typically made in a crockpot by the home soapmaker, you can also speed up the process by soaping at higher temperatures. You heat your oils to roughly 240 , add your lye solution when still hot, and leverage the high temperatures to accelerate the saponification process. Do not attempt this without further research and understanding of the process!

**LTHP** - Low Temperature Hot Process. This is the opposite of HTHP where you keep the temperature low while making your soap, but hotter than CP soapmaking.

**OO** - Olive Oil

**Partial Gel** - When making CP soap, it is possible for only the center of the loaf to enter the gel phase. This results in a ring of darker colored soap in the center. This can be a design feature, or an unwanted issue.

**Rebatch** - Soap scraps, or otherwise unwanted soap, can be saved and rebatched into new soap. There are many methods ranging from simply melting down existing soap to incorporating the old bits into new oils.

**Tare Weight** - this is the empty weight of your vessel. It's useful to record this weight so you can subtract it from the weight of your filled vessel to calculate the weight of the contents.

# Happy Soaping!

I hope you find as much joy in making soap as I have. For me, the journey started as a science experiment while homeschooling my children and has evolved into a sustainable business, gained me dear friends, and helped me find a deeper love for nature and science.

When you make your soaps and reach landmarks along your own journey, I hope you will share them with me and all of our soapy friends. You can email, post comments on my website, or tag me on your favorite social media platform, or maybe I'll see you in a soapmaking group on Facebook.

I can't wait to see what you create and to continue learning with you!

Happy soaping!

Kandra Churchwell
www.SoapyFriends.com
@mysoapyfriends